Turn your artwork into animated films! Here is a truly innovative coloring book designed to bring pictures to life with the help of a free Blink Book app.

MEDIA CONTACT:
Jamie Tan, Publicist
t. 617.588.4523
e. jamie.tan@candlewick.com

Become an artist and filmmaker in one go with an exciting new twist on the coloring book. Kids are invited to color in the pictures, take photos of them using a free Blink Book app (downloaded separately onto a phone or tablet), and watch them turn into animated films . . . as easy as color, snap, app! With sixteen spreads to color, users are able to produce sixteen animated episodes totaling eight minutes' worth of video—and will be thrilled to play the role of creator in this cutting-edge blend of art and technology.

Claire Faÿ is a French artist and author. She is the founder of Editions Animées, a publishing start-up that creates digital technology to enhance our relationship with the traditional book.

MARKETING   **Online consumer advertising** | **Social media campaign** | **Virtual display copy**

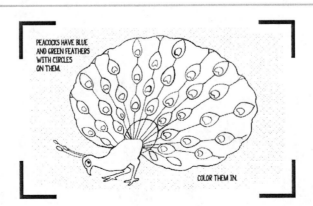

Color, Snap, App!
My First Animated Coloring Book
written and illustrated by Claire Faÿ
Activity book
13 x 9 1/16   32 pages
Ages 5–9
Kindergarten–Grade 4
Digital artwork
July

ISBN: 978-0-7636-9347-3
$9.99 ($10.99 CAN)

COLOR IN THE BOY.
WHAT COLOR ARE HIS CLOTHES?

COLOR IN THE HOUSE. DRAW SOME TREES AND FLOWERS.

MALE BIRDS OF PARADISE HAVE BRIGHTLY COLORED FEATHERS.
THE FEMALES ARE MORE PLAIN. COLOR IN THE BIRDS.

DRAW SOME SPOTS ON THE JAGUAR'S COAT.

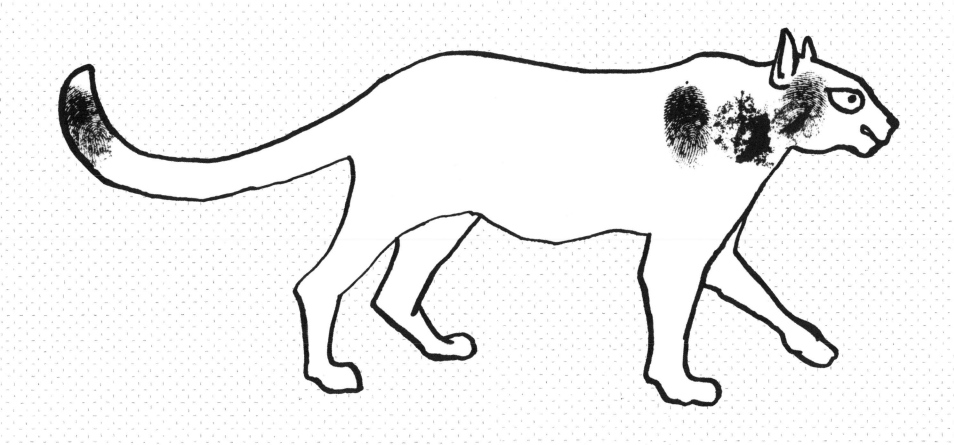

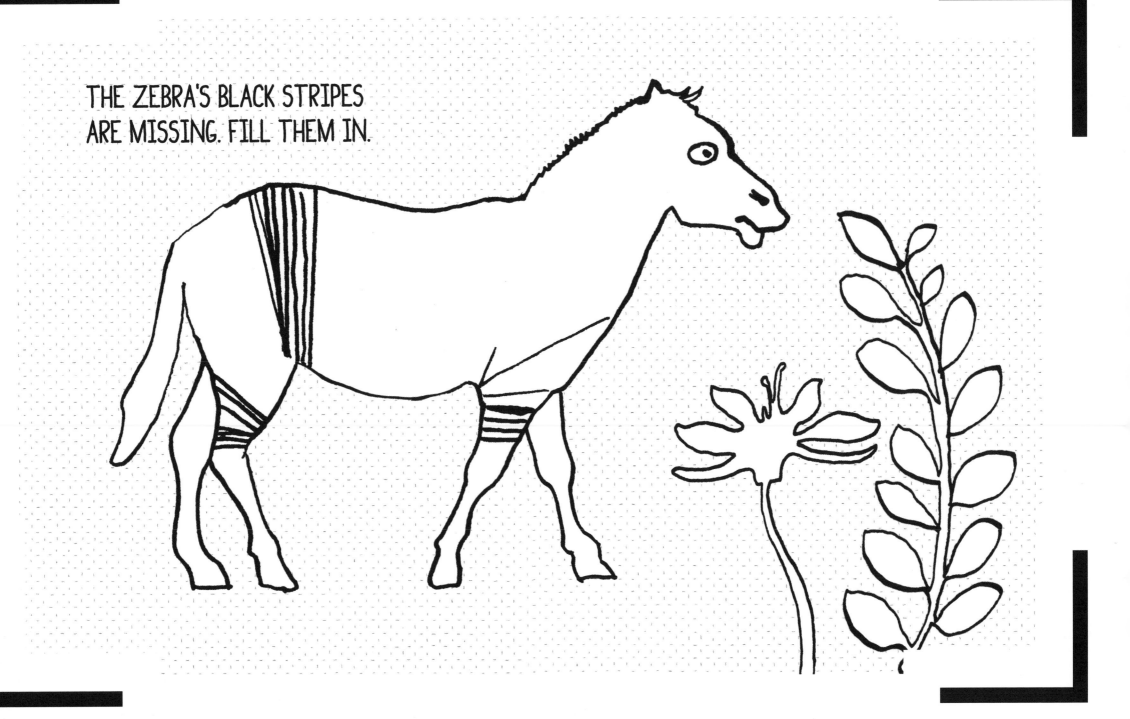

PEACOCKS HAVE BLUE
AND GREEN FEATHERS
WITH CIRCLES
ON THEM.

COLOR THEM IN.

COLOR IN THE TAPIRS. THE ADULTS ARE PLAIN
AND THE BABIES HAVE SPOTS AND STRIPES.

SCRIBBLE IN THE STOAT'S FUR.
USE A LIGHT OR DARK COLOR.

COLOR IN THE BAT.

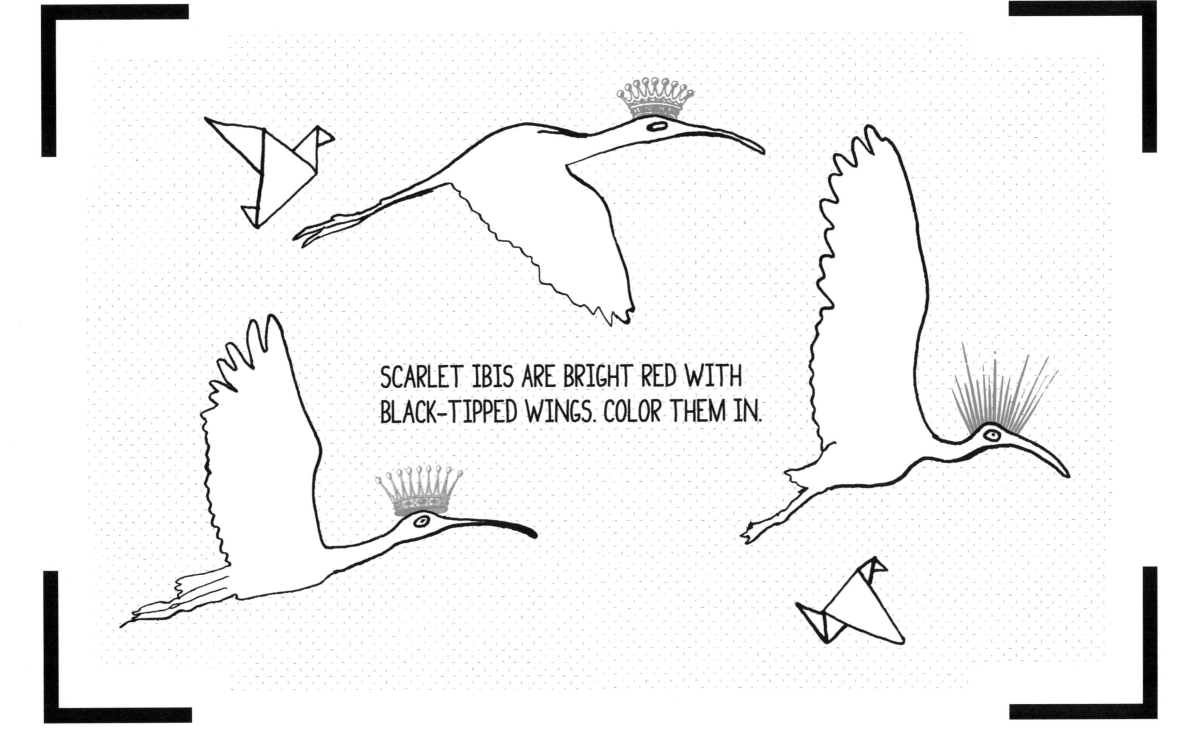

SCARLET IBIS ARE BRIGHT RED WITH BLACK-TIPPED WINGS. COLOR THEM IN.

COLOR IN THE MALE BIRD OF PARADISE'S BRIGHT WINGS.

CAN YOU DECORATE THE
BUTTERFLY'S WINGS?

HOW MANY MORE GEOMETRIC SHAPES
CAN YOU DRAW ON THE SNAKE?

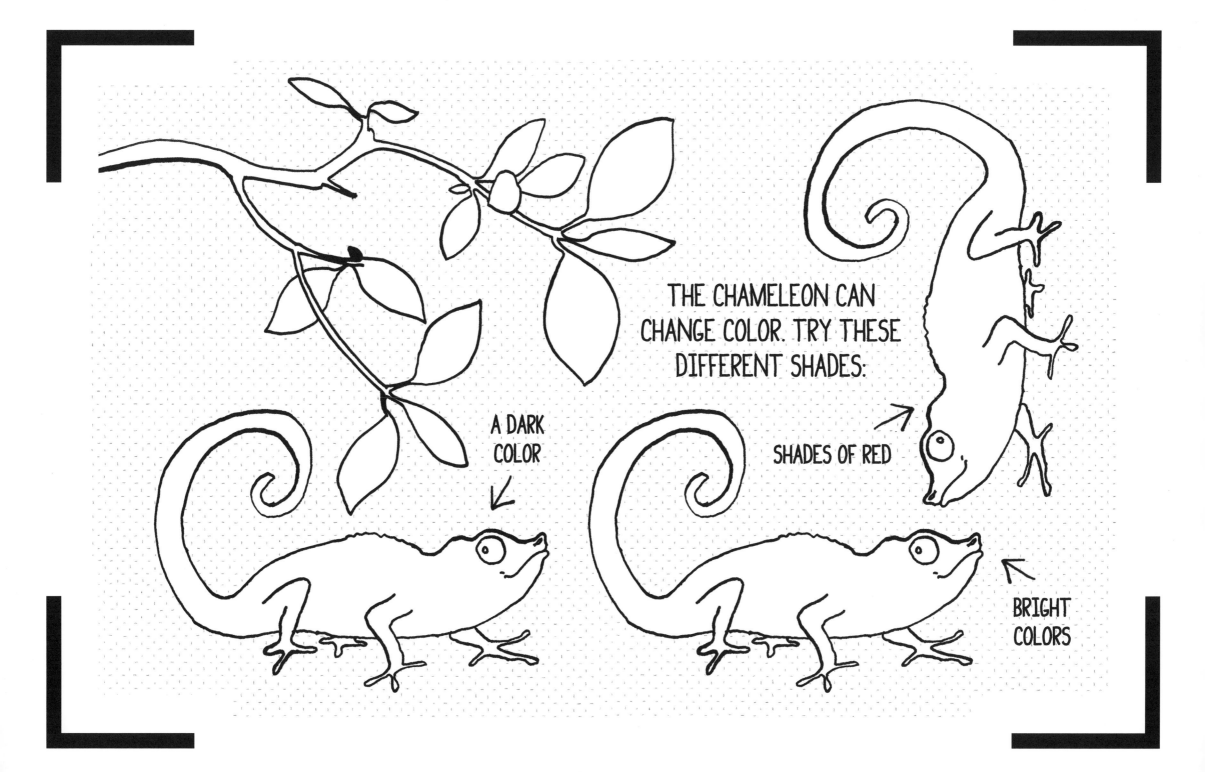

THE CHAMELEON CAN CHANGE COLOR. TRY THESE DIFFERENT SHADES:

A DARK COLOR

SHADES OF RED

BRIGHT COLORS